the Pascale Method

FOR BEGINNING VIOLIN

Written and illustrated by
Susan A. Pascale

For my family and friends, with gratitude, and, for all my teachers -

• The teachers who taught me how to play the violin

• My three children's many music teachers I observed during their years of lessons

• The music teachers that I've worked with through the years, and of course,

• My most important teachers - my students

BOOK
Art Direction and Graphic Design: Tracy Chiang
Cover Design: Lynn Salazar
Editor: Cathy Perlmutter

DVD
Executive Producer: A.J. Pascale
Director: Tracy Chiang
Editor: David W. Foster
Voices: A.J. Pascale and Susan Pascale
Mrs. Pascale's students: Isabela Butler, Andrés Engleman, Isabella Realzola
Quintet performers: Ashley Mok, Reo Snyder, Emma Phillips, Jenna Pascale, Sebastian Salazar
Music coach: Zach Dellinger
Music performed: El Toro by Don Brubaker
'4 Step Left Hand' background music: Turkey in the Straw (traditional), performed by
Ariana Solotoff, Jenna Pascale, Sebastian Salazar, Zach Dellinger, Susan Pascale

For press inquiries and free downloads for teachers and directors, go to
PascaleMethod.com

SECOND PRINTING, 2013
Printed in the USA by Westcott Press, CA

ISBN 9780967513713
Pascale, Susan
The Pascale Method for Beginning Violin with Stickers and DVD/Susan A. Pascale

PASCALE METHOD

Table of Contents

Lesson One

Lesson Two

Lesson Three

Lesson Four

Lesson Five

Lesson Six

Lesson Seven

Lesson Eight

Lesson Nine

Lesson Ten

Lesson Eleven

Lesson Twelve

The Caboose

Glossary - Pascale Method

Introduction

Welcome! And congratulations on your decision to learn the Pascale Method for Beginning Violin.

The Pascale Method is an innovative, step-by-step approach which addresses the physical, mental and emotional aspects of playing the violin. Through detailed directions, fun exercises, and a positive reward system, students master skills quickly and easily, and are motivated to continue.

I did not set out to create a method for violin instruction, let alone to become a full time violin teacher. It happened out of necessity. I'm a violinist with an art degree. When my son and daughter were very young, I was a single working mother, and couldn't afford music lessons – so I taught my children, myself. Because I had been a professional, I knew what a good violinist was supposed to look and sound like. This method evolved from over ten years of teaching, research, and trial and error.

In 2001, we moved from the cultural mecca of New York – where my second grader, Ariana, played violin in her elementary school orchestra – to a place in California where arts programs had been slashed, and there were no strings programs for my kids. Desperate for my daughter to have a group, I offered free violin lessons. Twenty-five students signed up, and three months later, we had an all-violin orchestra. Eventually we added other instruments and grew quickly into a flourishing strings program with hundreds of students and an award-winning children's orchestra.

I wish I had this book when I started out!

Susan Pascale

Susan Pascale

PASCALE METHOD

Who Can Use the Pascale Method?

First and foremost, the Pascale Method is for young beginners. The most difficult tasks are introduced first, and are broken down to their simplest form. The exercises are so easy and fun that anyone over 3½ years old can do them (although I recommend 4½ as the minimum age for violin, with a prerequisite of piano).

Along with young children, the Pascale Method is for:

- **BEGINNERS** of any age
- **TEACHERS**, beginning or experienced, who want to augment their skills
- **VIOLINISTS** who want to teach
- **PARENTS** of violin students
- **ANYONE** who would like to build a strings program, school-based or private

If you apply the method diligently, using the DVD, the Sticker Buddies 12 Lesson Pak, as well as this workbook, the result will be players with good form, relaxed disposition, beautiful tone, and a basic knowledge of theory and music, in a relatively short amount of time.

A special note to teachers:
For updates and useful information visit PascaleMethod.com.

PASCALE METHOD

Pascale Method Program Components:
I. THIS WORKBOOK
II. DVD
III. STICKER BUDDIES 12 LESSON PAK

I. THIS WORKBOOK

There are 12 numbered weekly lessons. Each includes:
- A Practice Assignment Sheet. Students check off each exercise as they practice.
- A Daily Practice Puzzle, found at the bottom of each assignment.

The Glossary. It contains exercises and musical definitions.

Throughout the book,
- **Bold** words refer to the exercises, which are found in the Glossary and on the DVD.
- *Italicized* words are found in the Glossary.

II. DVD

When you see this camera symbol , go to the DVD for a demonstration of the exercise.

III. STICKER BUDDIES 12 LESSON PAK (found at the back of this book)

Contains useful tools, like fingerboard tapes, finger pals, and wrist helpers. There are also practice incentives, such as collectible stickers and reward badges.
- Use the Chapter Tabs to mark the beginning of each chapter.
- Colorize your book by using the large round Color Sticks, whenever you see a circled drawing.

Let's get started!

Now insert your DVD and select "Watch this First." See you there!

PASCALE METHOD

What You Need for Class

CHECKLIST

____ **VIOLIN**
Properly sized, teacher approved.

____ **SHOULDER REST**
Adjustable brands are best.

____ **MUSIC STAND**
Find one to fit your budget and needs.

____ **PASCALE METHOD WORKBOOK**
Be sure to bring it to every lesson.

____ **DVD**
Found inside the back cover of this book.

____ **CRAYONS OR PENCILS**
Red, yellow, blue, green, and brown for
Theory Workshops.

Lesson One
Let's Get Started!

Before class begins, have your teacher place the fingerboard tapes onto your violin. (Tapes can be found in each of the 12 Lesson Sticker Buddies, found at the back of this book.)

In this lesson you will take a trip around the violin! Learning the parts of the violin is very important because we'll be referring to them throughout the course. Also, we will learn how to read music and even begin playing, starting with *pizzicato*.

The Pascale Method requires daily practice! Each day, on your Practice Assignment Sheet, make a check on the line provided to the left of the numbered exercise. Ideally, you should have 7 check marks for each exercise by the end of the week. Where there is a short line (as in Lesson One, exercise 1), it is only necessary to practice the exercise one time.

To add to the fun, use the Sticker Buddies - Daily Practice Puzzle Pieces to fill in the empty chart located at the bottom of each Practice Assignment. Match the numbers on the scrambled stickers to the numbers on the chart.

If you practice every day, a surprise picture will appear!

Take Note!

CREATE ROUTINE

1. Find a place in your home to call your 'practice area'. Keep your music stand set up 24/7.

2. Try to practice at the same time every day.

3. Parents closely supervise each practice session.

Lesson One
Practice Assignment #1

Check off each exercise as you practice EVERY DAY. Refer to the DVD when you see this icon: 📹

_____1. Teach someone in your household the 'Parts of the Violin'. (Page 1-3)

_____2. Read 'How to Take Care of Your Violin'. (Page 1-3)

_____ 3. **Hold Your Violin Correctly.** 📹

Take these 8 easy steps:

1) Place your violin in *rest position*.
2) Start with your feet together, then fan them open to make a V. Your right foot steps sideways. Your feet end up hip distance apart.
3) Place your left thumb on the *back button* of the violin. Swish the thumb forward, with fingers facing forward, parallel to the *fingerboard*.
4) Rotate the violin upside down (to the right). Show the teacher your violin.
5) Standing tall, with your head facing forward, place the *bottom button* of the violin in your ear. Keep the violin in **Table Position**.
6) Slowly drop the violin until it lands on your shoulder.
7) Push the violin gently into your neck.
8) Take a deep breath, raise your chin straight up in the air, slowly turn your head towards the scroll and drop your chin down gently on the *chin rest*.

Now you are in *correct violin position*!
Remember, holding the violin correctly is key to building a good player.

4. **Theory Workshop. Complete the worksheets.** (Pages 1-4, 5, 8, 9, 12)

____Meet the Family ____This is a Staff ____Find Your Notes ____Draw Your Notes ____Name Your Notes

_____ 5. Holding your violin correctly, **Pluck** notes on Flashcards #1-4. (Pages 1-6, 7, 10, 11) 📹

Good **Pizzicato** *position looks like this:*
a. Place your thumb on the corner of the *fingerboard*.
b. Circle your first finger around making a "doorway".
c. Make contact with the string one inch from the bottom of the *fingerboard* and gently **Pluck** each string with the padded part of your index finger.

_____ 6. Cut out flashcards and memorize the names of the 4 basic notes. (Pages 1-6, 7, 10, 11)

Congratulations on completing your first Practice Assignment!
You've earned a Reward Badge from Lesson One Sticker Buddies.

PIZZICATO MEANS PLUCK

DAY 1	DAY 2	DAY 3	DAY 4	DAY 5	DAY 6	DAY 7

PASCALE METHOD

Lesson One
Fun Facts
About the Violin

PARTS OF THE VIOLIN:

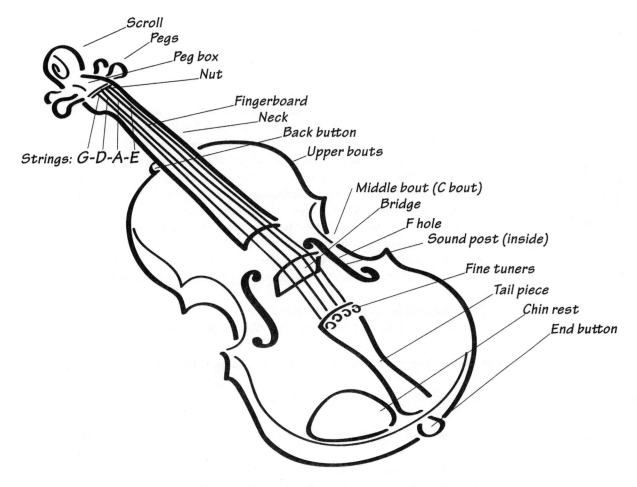

Scroll
Pegs
Peg box
Nut
Fingerboard
Neck
Back button
Upper bouts
Strings: G-D-A-E
Middle bout (C bout)
Bridge
F hole
Sound post (inside)
Fine tuners
Tail piece
Chin rest
End button

HOW TO TAKE CARE OF YOUR VIOLIN:
ALWAYS...

- Dust it daily with a soft cloth.
- Keep it away from young siblings and pets.
- Rest it in its case during practice breaks. (Never on a chair or floor.)
- Never place it face down, which could damage the bridge.
- Never leave it in the car, especially on very hot or cold days.
- Never touch the bow hair.
- Never drop your violin. Beginners practice on a carpet!

PASCALE METHOD

Lesson One
Theory Workshop
Meet the Family

Directions:

PRACTICE WRITING YOUR FOUR BASIC NOTES

Here is Your FiRST COLOR STICK. FiND THE CORRESPONDiNG STICKER iN Lesson One STICKER BUDDiES.

G FOR GRANDPA (HE LIVES IN THE BASEMENT)

D FOR DADDY

A FOR AUNTIE

E... MOMMY SEES A MOUSE!

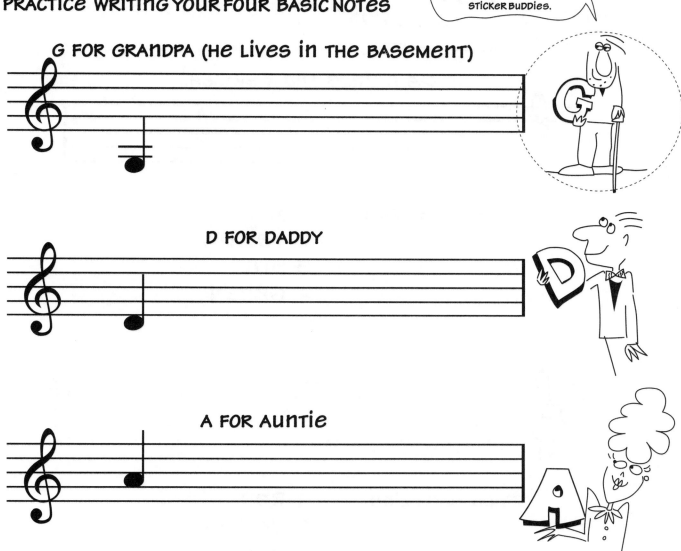

PASCALE METHOD

Lesson One
Theory Workshop
This is a Staff

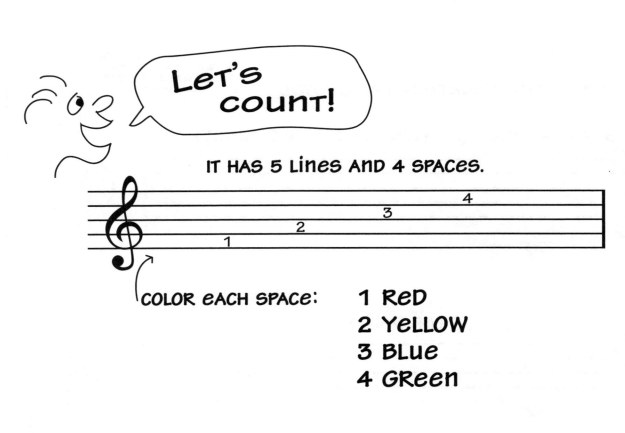

IT HAS 5 LINES AND 4 SPACES.

COLOR EACH SPACE: 1 RED
2 YELLOW
3 BLUE
4 GREEN

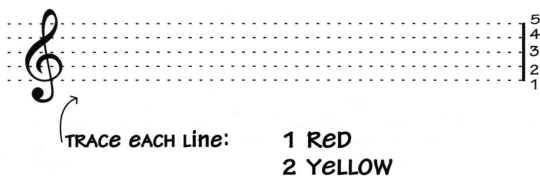

TRACE EACH LINE: 1 RED
2 YELLOW
3 BLUE
4 GREEN
5 BROWN

PASCALE METHOD

Lesson One
Learn to Read
Flashcards #1

G NOTE
Count and pluck "one-two-three-four"

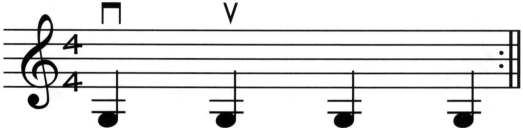

G IS THE LOWEST NOTE ON THE VIOLIN.

Learn your G note!

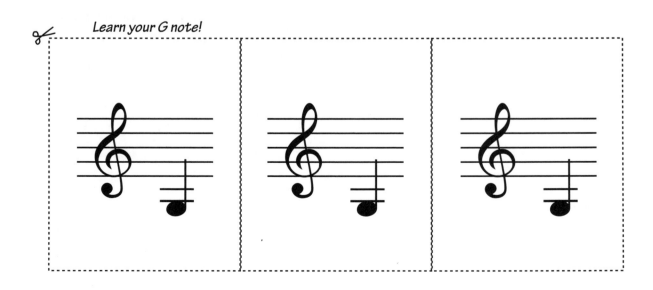

Lesson One
Learn to Read
Flashcards #2

D NOTE
Count and pluck "one-two-three-four"

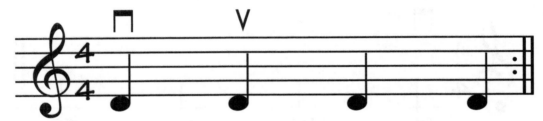

PARENT MAY POINT TO EACH NOTE WHILE CHILD IS PLAYING.

Learn your D note!

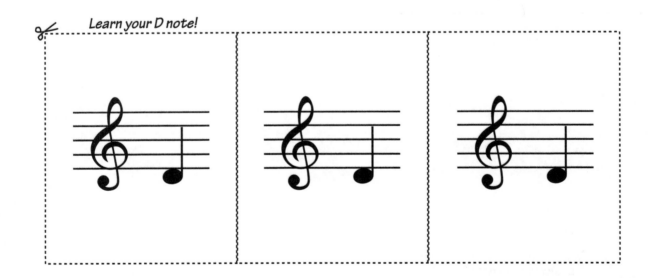

Lesson One
Theory Workshop
Find Your Notes

HEY LOOK!
THEY ARE ALL ON
THE SPACES.

☐ COLOR THE A NOTE RED

☐ COLOR THE D NOTE YELLOW

☐ COLOR THE E NOTE GREEN

☐ COLOR THE G NOTE BLUE

NOW FIND THEM ON YOUR VIOLIN!

☐ CIRCLE THE TREBLE CLEFF BLUE

☐ CIRCLE THE BAR LINE RED

☐ CIRCLE THE REPEAT SIGN GREEN

☐ COUNT THE MEASURES_____

PASCALE METHOD

Lesson One
Theory Workshop
Draw Your Notes & Treble CLef

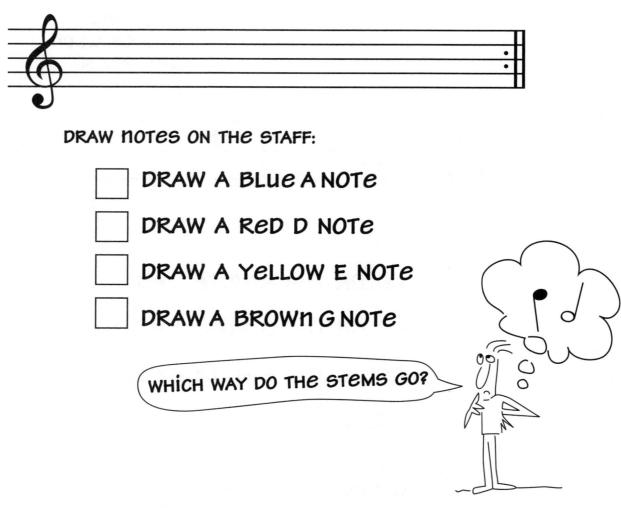

DRAW NOTES ON THE STAFF:

- [ ] DRAW A BLUE A NOTE
- [ ] DRAW A RED D NOTE
- [ ] DRAW A YELLOW E NOTE
- [ ] DRAW A BROWN G NOTE

WHICH WAY DO THE STEMS GO?

DRAW YOUR TREBLE CLEF:

PASCALE METHOD

Lesson One
Learn to Read
Flashcards #3

A NOTE
Count and pluck "one-two-three-four"

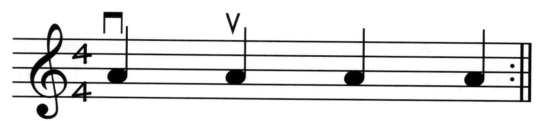

DON'T FORGET TO REPEAT!

Learn your A note!

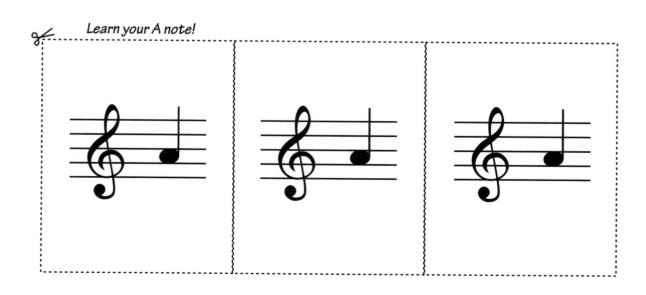

Lesson One
Learn to Read
Flashcards #4

E NOTe
Count and pluck "one-two-three-four"

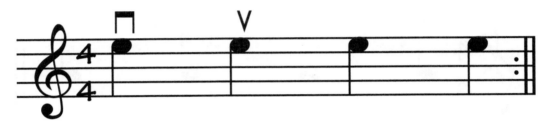

WHen You ARe PLuCKinG, YouR inDeX FinGeR MAKeS A DOORWAY!

Learn your E note!

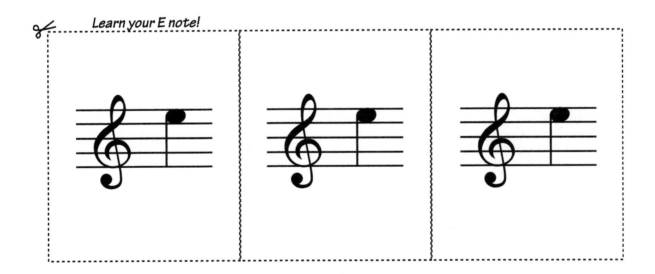

Lesson One
Theory Workshop
Name Your Notes

WRITE THE LETTER NAMES OF THE OPEN STRING NOTES:

PASCALE METHOD

Lesson Two
Left Hand &
Introducing the Bow

This week, you will give yourself a hand—your left hand! Now that you can hold your violin, you're ready. You must follow the step-by-step instructions exactly to create proper form. Avoiding bad habits from the very beginning will help with *intonation*, and accelerate progress, which will lead to playing fun and varied pieces.

You will also be introduced to the gang of characters who will help you learn to hold the bow correctly.

Take Note!

FOR PARENTS

1. Help your child take responsibility for their practice. Provide them with a "special pencil" to check off each exercise as they complete it. Create your own reward box or

2. a treasure chest full of fun prizes for practice incentives.

PASCALE METHOD

Lesson Two
Practice Assignment #2

_____ 1. Take the steps to **Hold Your Violin Correctly.** 🔲

_____ 2. Make a **Stop Sign.** 🔲
    a) Find your left hand index finger. With a black marker, color in the third crease down from the top.
    b) While holding your violin correctly, make a flat open left hand, (**Stop Sign**) and line up your black line with the bottom of the thickness of the *fingerboard.*
    c) Point your fingers to the ceiling. Now lay the fingers back at a 45 degree angle. This is **Fingers Lay in the Sun.**

_____ 3. **Tik Tok** your elbow in then out. (5x) 🔲

_____ 4. **Find Your Y** by bending your index finger. 🔲

_____ 5. **First Finger Goes to the Gym.** 🔲
    a) Line up your **Stop Sign, Fingers Lay in the Sun, Tik Tok** your elbow in
    b) **Find Your Y**; bend your first finger onto the first tape on your E string
    c) Give your finger a workout, move it up and down on your E string (6x)

_____ 6. In good **Pizzicato** position, practice 'Learn to Read'. (Pages 2-4, 2-6) 🔲
Look for the "doorway" shape made when your thumb leans on the corner of the *fingerboard* and your index finger circles around to **Pluck** the string.

_____ 7. Get to know your bow.
    a) Read: Fun Facts About the Bow (Page 2-3)
    b) Tighten and loosen your bow
    c) Read: Fun Facts About Rosin (Page 2-5)
    d) Rosin your bow

_____ 8. Introducing the **Train Gang!**
Meet them at The Caboose. (Pages C-1, 2, 3, 4) 🔲

In this lesson get to know:
  1) Mr. Engineer: He sits down to drive the train
  2) Mr. Conductor: He circles around to collect the tickets

You will only place <u>two fingers</u> on the bow this week. (6x)

_____ 9. Review your flashcards from Lesson One.
  • Memorize the note names and play them on your violin.

Nice meeting you too

Place a Daily Practice Puzzle Piece from Lesson Two Sticker Buddies and see what appears!
(*If you practice every day.*)

DAY 1   DAY 2   DAY 3   DAY 4   DAY 5   DAY 6   DAY 7

I ♡ 2 PRACTICE ▷

PASCALE METHOD

Lesson Two
Fun Facts
About the Bow

PARTS OF THE BOW:

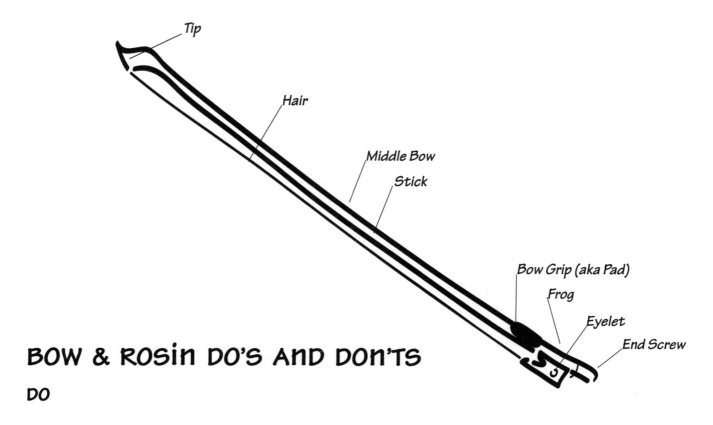

Tip

Hair

Middle Bow

Stick

Bow Grip (aka Pad)

Frog

Eyelet

End Screw

BOW & ROSIN DO'S AND DON'TS

DO

- Loosen your bow after each use, to prevent hairs from stretching.
- Place your bow back in the case after every use.
  Clean your bow and violin with a microfiber cloth after each time you play.
  This prevents rosin buildup.
- Be stingy with rosin. Over-rosining can be hazardous to your sound.

DON'T

- Do not touch, grab, or stroke your bow hairs. The oils and dirt from your hands will ruin the bow.
- Never leave your bow on the floor or on a chair.
- You had better not poke or whack your friends, siblings or pets with it. Bows are fragile, and will break at the tip!
- Leaning on it like a cane, or hitting it on the floor when frustrated, will also lead to a broken bow.

PASCALE METHOD

Lesson Two
Learn to Read
The Two Middle Strings
Basic Notes

PLUCK YOUR NOTES

♩ - *These are quarter notes. Each note receives one count.*

⊓ - *Means down bow. The direction from frog to tip.*

∨ - *Means up bow. The direction from tip to frog.*

D IS FOR DADDY STRING

A IS FOR AUNTIE STRING

D 'n A

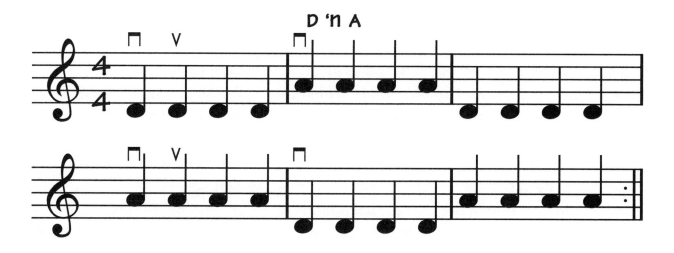

PASCALE METHOD

Lesson Two
Fun Facts
About Rosin

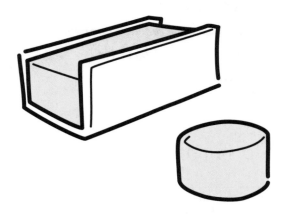

DEFINITION: ros·in [pronounced roz-in]

1. **NOUN:** *The translucent, fragmented resin from pine trees: used for rubbing on violin bows.*

2. **VERB** *to cover or rub with rosin.*

WITHOUT ROSIN, YOUR VIOLIN WON'T MAKE A SOUND.

Rosin comes in different types and grades, from dark to extra pale, ranging from $1.50 to $38 and up. It's made from resin collected from 150 different types of pine trees around the world. There are many unique recipes for rosin, which the makers keep top secret. Professional violinists are always searching for the ideal rosin, which has to do with the level of stickiness. Kids tend to judge rosin by its cover. 'Pop-up' rosin (which we nicknamed 'secret agent' rosin) is popular among preteens. I personally like 'mini-rosins' for my students - they fit comfortably in little fingers and aren't too costly when children accidently drop them, causing them to shatter into many unusable pieces.

PASCALE METHOD

Lesson Two
Learn to Read
The Two Outer Strings
Basic Notes

Lesson Three

Left Hand - Bow Hold - Bow Arm

In this lesson, we're continuing with the left hand. We will meet our Finger Pals. For extra support you can peel off your **4 Step Left Hand** badge (from Sticker Buddies - Lesson Three) and place it strategically on your music stand or in your practice area.

You'll meet the rest of your Train Gang who will help you hold your bow correctly. If you can master the bow hold this week, you'll be well on your way to playing!

A good bow arm starts with **Square Position**. With your violin correctly placed, you will learn the **Airplane Wing**. Remember to always stand tall and keep your muscles relaxed. This will help build good form which will lead to playing with a beautiful sound.

Take Note!

4 STEP LEFT HAND

1. Make a **Stop Sign** - line it up

2. Fingers back, **Lay in the Sun**

3. Tik-Tok elbow, almost done...

4. **Walk Your Fingers**, one by one!

PASCALE METHOD

Lesson Three
Practice Assignment #3

_____ 1. Meet Your **Finger Pal** and use it throughout this lesson! o📷
   Finger Pals will help you play with a good left hand. Peel a pal from your Sticker Buddies - Lesson Three. Circle your index finger around, and place the pal vertically on the nail, so it can look you in the eye when you're playing.

_____ 2. Take the steps to **Hold Your Violin Correctly.** o📷

_____ 3. Peel your **4 Step Left Hand** badge from Sticker Buddies - Lesson Three, and place it in your practice area. Refer to it throughout this course. Now follow these steps:
   1) Make a **Stop Sign,** line it up.
      Remember, fingers point to the ceiling.
   2) Fingers back, **Lay in the Sun.**
      Fingers tilt back in a 45degree angle. Look for the straight line your hand and forearm make.
   3) **Tik Tok** elbow, almost done...
      Move your hand and elbow in as one unit.
   4) **Walk Your Fingers, Start With One.**
      Move your first finger from the E to G strings. Make sure your **Finger Pal** is looking at you.

_____ 4. Find Your **Finger Table.** o📷
   Place your first finger on the E string and **Find Your Y.** Is your **Finger Pal** looking at you? This is a **Finger Table.**

_____ 5. **Walk Your Fingers** 1-2-3 on each string, starting on E string. o📷
   Tik-Tok your elbow in as you move toward the G. Use your **Finger Pal, Find Your Y** with your first finger. Can you find your **Finger Table** on each string?

_____ 6. **Pluck** your Learn to Read Quarter Notes & Quarter Rests. (Pages 3-3 & 3-6)

_____ 7. Get to know the whole **Train Gang!** Meet at The Caboose. (Page C-4)
   Say your five steps out loud (6x). This is how you make your bow hold.

_____ 8. Ride the **Elevator.** (Page C-5) o📷

_____ 9. Find **Square Position** on the D string. o📷
   Before you begin, place a _center dot_ on your bow. (From Sticker Buddies)
   • Take the steps to **Hold Your Violin Correctly.** Place your violin in **Table Position.**
   • Place the bow's _center dot_ on the _sounding point_ of your violin.
   • Check that your nose is looking down on the bridge, and left foot lines up with the _scroll._
   • See the shape your arm makes - it's a square!

_____ 10. **Airplane Wing** o📷
   Find your **Square Position.** Starting with your bow on the G string, slowly drop your 'wing' from G to E. Your hand and elbow stay together.

_____ 11. Practice your Level 1 Rhythm Cards. (Page 3-4)

Cut them out and have the whole family play along!

DAY 1	DAY 2	DAY 3	DAY 4	DAY 5	DAY 6	DAY 7

PASCALE METHOD

Lesson THREE
Learn to Read
Quarter Notes & Quarter Rests

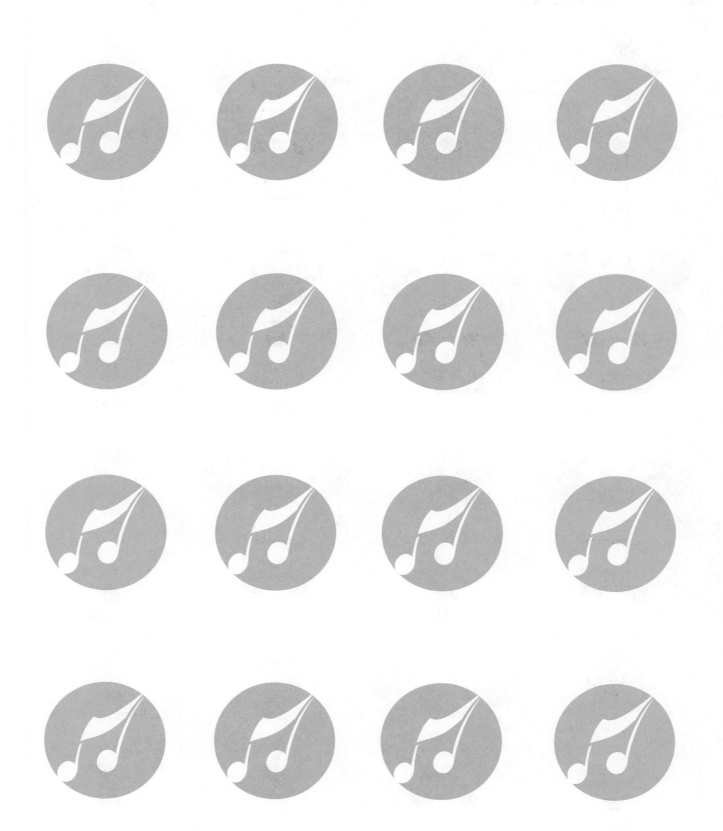

Lesson Three
Learn to Read
Eighth Notes, Quarter Notes
& Quarter Rests

 = Ti-Ti

 = Tah

= Rest

Fine!

 'FINE' MEANS ALL DONE!

PASCALE METHOD

Lesson Four
Let the Bowing Begin!

This week, in addition to reviewing what you've learned, we'll be focusing on your bow arm, specifically the wrist, which drives the bow fingers. The exercises here are designed to keep your bow nice and straight. Up to now we've only plucked. Now we'll review the exercises that you plucked, and play them with the bow!

Take Note!

PRACTICE, PRACTICE, BREAK?

Having an off day? Shorten today's practice. Choose three or four favorite exercises. Remember, it's the every day practice that's most important.

BOWING is NOT FOR WIMPS!

PASCALE METHOD

Lesson Four

Practice Assignment #4

_____ 1. Take the steps to **Hold Your Violin Correctly.** Watch your feet!

_____ 2. Work with the **Train Gang** to hold your bow correctly.
    Place your bow fingers one at a time. Say each step out loud. Repeat this (8x)

_____ 3. Do **Pinky Push-ups.** (5x)

_____ 4. Ride the **Elevator** ↕ Find the 'n' and 'u' shapes your wrist makes. (4x)
    Now, try it on the violin! ↔ We call this **Elevator on the Violin.** (Do this 4x on D string)

_____ 5. Before you begin this exercise, affix a _wrist helper_ from Sticker Buddies - Lesson Four.
    Find Your Shapes on each string (2x):

             Square   Big Triangle   Square   Small Triangle

    Look at Your Watch as your bow travels an _up bow_ motion (tip to frog).

        I heard 'UP BOW' means tip to FROG

_____ 6. Get into **Square Position.**
    Do the **Airplane Wing** on all of your strings.
    Be sure your elbow and hand stay together!

_____ 7. Go to **The Wall.** (Page C-7)
    Peel a _center dot_ (From Sticker Buddies) and affix it to the
    middle bow. Stay in the _center dot_ area as you play and chant
    "I love to play my violin" on the G-D-A-E strings.

_____ 8. Refer to your **4 Step Left Hand** badge and **Walk Your Fingers** 1, 2 & 3
    on the G-D-A-E strings. (Do this 3x on each string.)

_____ 9. Using your bow, go back and practice all the exercises that you **Plucked.**
    (Pages 2-4 & 6 and Pages 3-3 & 6)

_____ 10. Practice your Level 1 Rhythm Cards. (from Lesson Three, Page 3-4)

DAY 1	DAY 2	DAY 3	DAY 4	DAY 5	DAY 6	DAY 7

Lesson Five

Mastering the Bow & Introducing Half Notes

You will begin to master the bow with the new exercises in this lesson. Pay special attention to make sure there is no tension in the wrist or fingers. We describe it this way: There is a motor in the wrist that drives the bow hand, and your fingers are on vacation. It's as if the fingers were passengers asleep in the back seat of a car - relaxed, carefree.

Place a wrist helper on your bow hand wrist this week. (Found in Sticker Buddies - Lesson Five.) This will give you a focal point to facilitate the bending movement.

Take Note!

Good Form +
Relaxed Disposition

= BEAUTIFUL SOUND

PASCALE METHOD

Lesson Five
Practice Assignment #5

_____ 1. Take the steps to **Hold Your Violin Correctly**. Get into **Table Position**. 📹

_____ 2. Saying the **Train Gang** steps out loud, make your bow hold. (5x) 📹

_____ 3. Do **Pinky Push-ups**. (5x) 📹

_____ 4. Make your bow hold 2x with your eyes closed. Do **Pinky Push-ups**. (2x) 📹

_____ 5. **Ride the Elevator** ↕ Find the 'n' and 'u' shapes your wrist makes. (4x) 📹
Now, try it on the violin! ↔ We call this **Elevator on the Violin**. (4x on G)

_____ 6. **On and Off the Train** (with stops): Exercise #1a, (3x) each string (Page C-6) 📹

_____ 7. Get into **Square Position** and find each bow level with your **Airplane Wing**. 📹
Your elbow and hand stay together. Try lifting from the forearm.

_____ 8. **Find Your Shapes:** □ ◣ □ ◿ (4x each string) 📹
Square   Big Triangle   Square   Small Triangle
Use a _wrist helper_ and **Look at Your Watch** on the _up bow_ motion.

_____ 9. _Sleeping Hand_ exercise. Find a _sleeping hand_ in your household.
It can be a parent, baby sister or your family pet.
Lift the hand up and down slowly (1x). How heavy does it feel?
Remember the feeling; it will help you play with a relaxed bow hold.

_____ 10. Go to **The Wall** and in **Square Position:** 📹
Make a **Stop Sign, Fingers Lay in the Sun, Tik Tok** your elbow in,
Play " I love to play my violin" on each string or make up a new song!

_____ 11. Practice your D scale. (Page 5-3)
Choose a **Finger Pal** to fit your mood and affix it to your left hand index fingernail.
Find Your Y and refer to the **4 Step Left Hand** badge!
Try practicing without the bow for the first two days.

_____ 12. Practice **Learn to Read Half Notes**. (Page 5-6)
Look for your _shapes_ when you do this exercise!

_____ 13. Practice **Level 2 Rhythm Cards**. (Page 5-4)

DAY 1	DAY 2	DAY 3	DAY 4	DAY 5	DAY 6	DAY 7

PASCALE METHOD

Lesson Five
Learn to Play Scales
D Scale

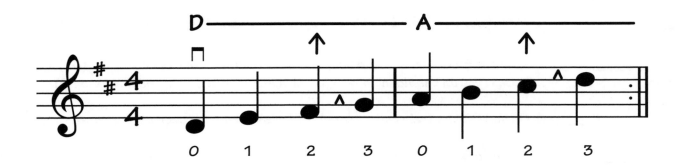

↑ THESE FINGERS ARE HIGH (ON THE TAPE).

∧ THESE FINGERS ARE TOUCHING.

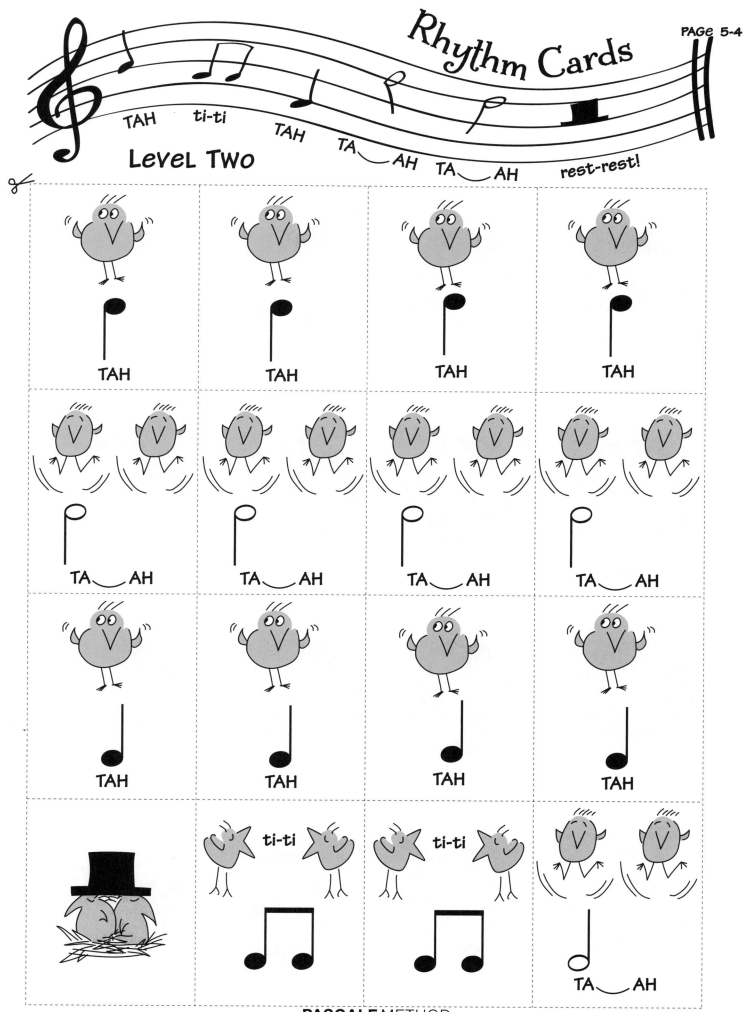

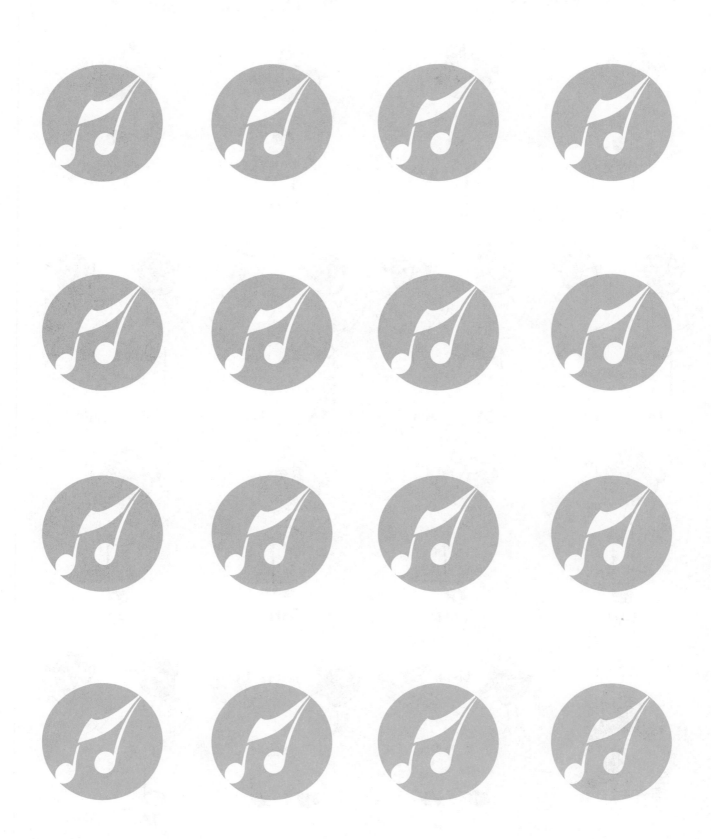

Lesson Five
Learn to Read
Half Notes

THE D STRING

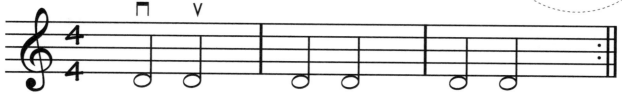

THE A STRING

THE G STRING

THE E STRING

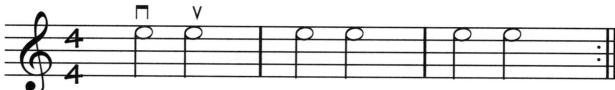

PASCALE METHOD

♩ = TA AH

Lesson Six

Stay the Course –
You're Halfway There!

At this point, you'll notice a repetition of exercises, along with some new ones. The quality of your practice for the remaining six lessons is crucial to a successful outcome! Remain diligent with your practicing, and thoughtful in your approach. Don't hesitate to go back and repeat previous assignments and review the exercises on the DVD.

Take Note!

How is learning to play the violin like building a house?

Both need to start with a GOOD FOUNDATION!

PASCALE METHOD

Lesson Six
Practice Assignment #6

_____ 1. Take the steps to **Hold Your Violin Correctly**. Get into **Table Position**. 📹

_____ 2. Using the **Train Gang** steps, Make your bow hold (4x) slowly and (3x) quickly.

_____ 3. Do **Pinky Push-Ups**. (8x) 📹

_____ 4. Ride the **Elevator** ↕ Find the 'n' and 'u' shapes your wrist makes. 📹
Now, try it on the violin! ↔ We call this **Elevator on the Violin**. (4x on D)

_____ 5. **Find Your Shapes**: ☐ ◺ ☐ ◹ 📹
Square Big Triangle Square Small Triangle

Use your _wrist helper_ to remind you to bend your wrist. You can say,
"Look at your watch, what time is it?" Do this (4x) on each string.

_____ 6. For this exercise, place a _center dot_ on your bow to assist your bow division. 📹
On and Off the Train (with stops): Exercise #1a, (3x) each string (Page C-6)
Counting Train Cars: Exercise #2, Count all the cars (2x), on each string (Page C-6)

_____ 7. From **Square Position** practice the **Airplane Wing** on all of your strings. 📹
Starting on G, feel the bow level as you drop to each string.

_____ 8. Go to **The Wall**. 📹
Place your bow using your _center dot_. Stay in the middle bow area while
you play and chant "I love to play my violin" on G-D-A-E strings. (Page C-7)

_____ 9. Practice **A Little Mozart**, Exercise #1. (Page 6-3)

_____ 10. Practice **Learn to Read**, Half Note Melodies. (Page 6-6)

_____ 11. Cut out, and practice Level 3 Rhythm Cards. (Page 6-4)

music to my ears...

| DAY 1 | DAY 2 | DAY 3 | DAY 4 | DAY 5 | DAY 6 | DAY 7 |

PASCALE METHOD

Lesson Six
Learn to Read!
A Little Mozart #1

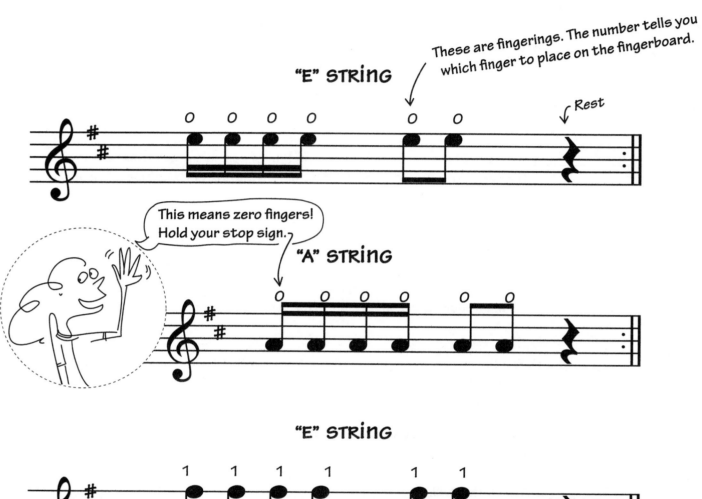

WALK THESE FINGERS 1-2-3 ON THE A STRING

PASCALE METHOD

Rhythm Cards

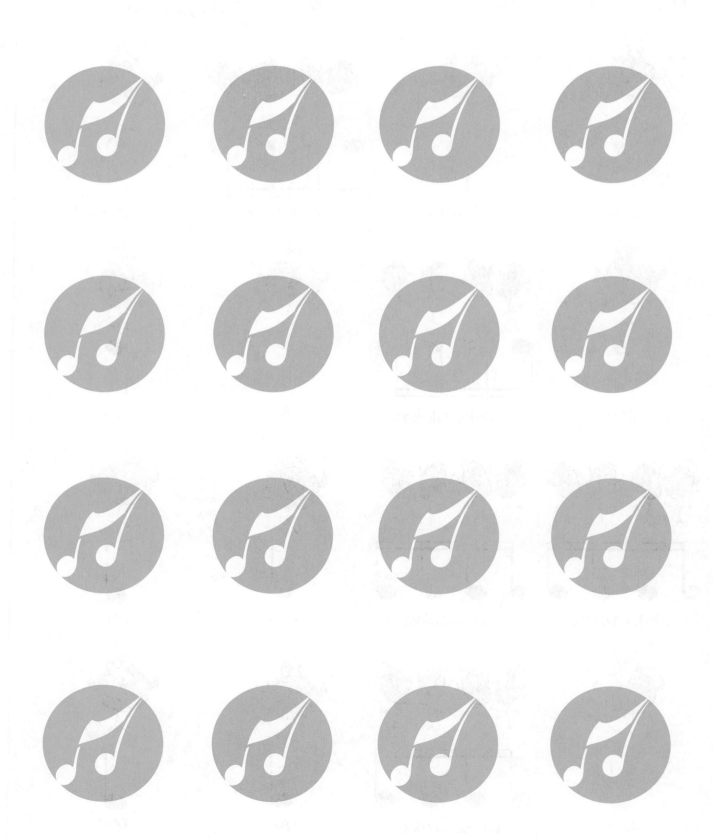

Lesson Six
Learn to Read
Half Note Melodies

PASCALE METHOD

Lesson Seven

Just Testing
& Developing Finger Dexterity

This lesson brings more dexterity with your right (bow) arm, as well as your left hand. We'll also test you on theory basics . Keep practicing every day – you'll build strength and confidence in your ability to play the violin!

Take Note!

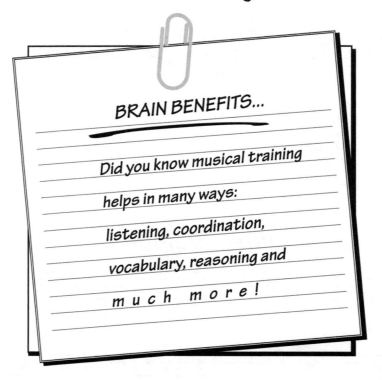

BRAIN BENEFITS...

Did you know musical training

helps in many ways:

listening, coordination,

vocabulary, reasoning and

m u c h   m o r e !

PASCALE METHOD

Lesson Seven
Practice Assignment #7

_____ 1. Take the steps to **Hold Your Violin Correctly.**

_____ 2. Practice your bow hold, saying the **Train Gang** steps. (Page C-6)
Say the steps out loud (4x), silently (2x), with your eyes closed. (3x)

_____ 3. a) Do the **Elevator** ↕ Make 'n' and 'u' shapes with your wrist.
b) Now, try it on the violin! ↔ (We call this **Elevator on the Violin.**)

_____ 4. **Find Your Shapes:** □ ◺ □ ◹ (3x each string)
Square Big Triangle Square Small Triangle

_____ 5. Do the **On and Off the Train** Exercise #1a on each string. (2x) (Page C-6)

_____ 6. Practice **Airplane Wing** on all strings. Elbow and hand stay together!

_____ 7. Place a _wrist helper_, and practice the **Two String Airplane:**

Be sure to look at your watch on the up bow motion!

LIFT ARM TO 'A' LEVEL
1 DROP ARM 3 BEND WRIST

_____ 8. Go to **The Wall.** Play this rhythm on G-D-A-E strings:

Practice **The Wall** exercise 7x this week and earn a badge for a job well done!

_____ 9. Using your **4 Step Left Hand** technique, practice your A scale. (Page 7-3)
a) without the bow (fingering only)
b) with the bow

_____ 10. Practice **A Little Mozart,** Exercise #2. (Page 7-4)

_____ 11. Do the **Compose and Play** worksheet. (Page 7-6)

_____ 12. Practice your **Level 3 Rhythm Cards.** (Page 6-4)

DAY 1 DAY 2 DAY 3 DAY 4 DAY 5 DAY 6 DAY 7

PASCALE METHOD

Lesson Seven
Learn to Play Scales
A Scale

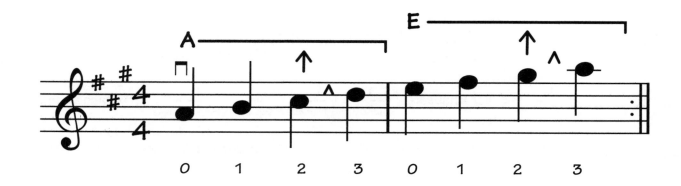

↑ THESE FINGERS ARE HIGH (ON THE TAPE).

^ THESE FINGERS ARE TOUCHING.

PASCALE METHOD

Lesson Seven
Learn to Read
A Little Mozart #2

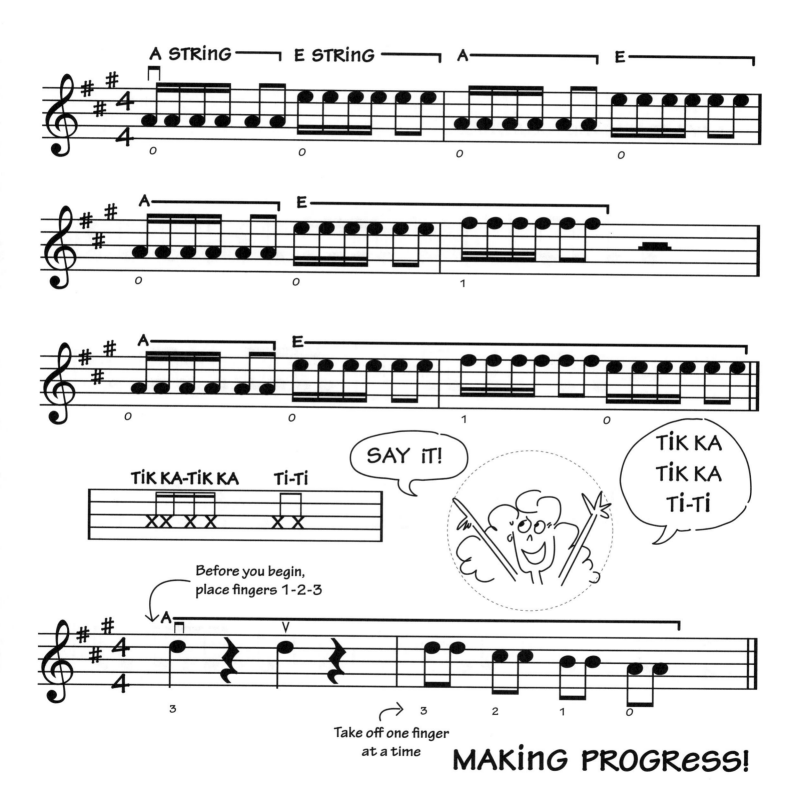

Lesson Seven
Got Rhythm?

SAY AND CLAP THE FOLLOWING:
Try setting your metronome to ♩ = 60

PASCALE METHOD

Lesson Seven
Theory Workshop
Compose & Play

COMPOSE A SONG WITH 4 QUARTER NOTES, USING G-D-A & E NOTES.

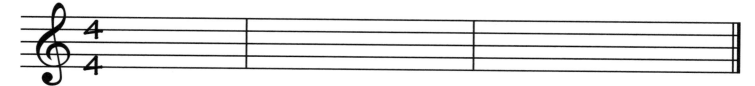

PRACTICE DRAWING YOUR G CLEF (ALSO CALLED TREBLE CLEF), QUARTER RESTS & HALF RESTS.

YOUR TURN

COMPOSE A SONG IN $\frac{4}{4}$ TIME WITH HALF NOTES & HALF RESTS.

ANSWER THE FOLLOWING:

How many measures are there in each song? _____

How many beats are in each measure? _____

NOW, PLAY YOUR 2 SONGS!
BE SURE TO BE IN GOOD VIOLIN POSITION.

PASCALE METHOD

Lesson Eight
It's Wall Week

This is a busy week. We are declaring it Wall Week! We understand that this exercise can be downright torturous; but the outcome is so great that we must do it. As a reward for your hard work on the wall, however, you get two badges for practicing it daily.

For train enthusiasts, you'll enjoy the Count Your Train Cars exercise. Mastering bow division as a beginner will help you use a lot of bow naturally, which is key to making a beautiful big sound.

Take Note!

PARENTS...

When in doubt, do not shout! Even when it feels like your child is not meeting your expectations, remain positive. Your child may just be going through a rough patch.

Lesson Eight
Practice Assignment #8

_____ 1. Take the steps to **Hold Your Violin Correctly.** Watch your feet placement! 📹

_____ 2. Make your bow hold slowly 4x and quickly 3x. Do **Pinky Push-ups.** (10 x) 📹

_____ 3. a) Do the **Elevator** ↕ Make 'n' and 'u' shapes with your wrist. 📹
    b) Now, try it on the violin! ↔ (We call this **Elevator** on the Violin.)

_____ 4. **Find Your Shapes:** □ ◺ □ ◹ 📹
    Square   Big Triangle   Square   Small Triangle

_____ 5. Place 4 *center dots* on your bow to help you plan your bow division. 📹
    On and Off the Train (with stops): Exercise #1a (2x) each string (Page C-6)
    Counting Train Cars: Exercise #2 Count all the cars (2x) each string (Page C-6)

_____ 6. From **Square Position** practice the **Airplane Wing** on all of your strings. 📹

ELBOW AND HAND STAY TOGETHER ♪♪♫♪

_____ 7. Place a *wrist helper* and practice the **Four String Airplane:**

    REVIEW: [music notation: LIFT ARM TO 'A' LEVEL, ① DROP ARM, ③ BEND WRIST]   CONTINUE WITH: [music notation]

_____ 8. Go to **The Wall** 8x this week and reward yourself with a badge! 📹
    Try one of these rhythms or make up your own!

    ♬♬♬ ♬♬♬ ♫♫ | ♬♬♬ ♫♫ 𝄾 | ♩ ♩ ♬♬♬

_____ 9. Practice your G scale. (Page 8-3)

_____ 10. Practice A Little Mozart, 3rd Finger Exercise. (Page 8-4)

_____ 11. Review A Little Mozart, Exercise #1 (Page 6-3) and #2. (Page 7-4)

_____ 12. Practice Learn to Read, Half Note Melodies, from Lesson Six. (Page 6-6)

_____ 13. Just Testing, Theory Review Test. (Page 8-4)

DAY 1	DAY 2	DAY 3	DAY 4	DAY 5	DAY 6	DAY 7

Lesson Eight
Learn to Play Scales

G Scale

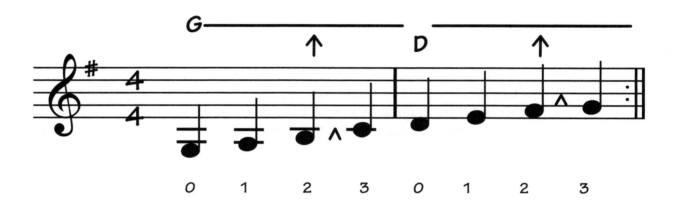

↑ THESE FINGERS ARE HIGH (ON THE TAPE).

∧ THESE FINGERS ARE TOUCHING.

PASCALE METHOD

Lesson Eight
Building Technique
A Little Mozart – 3rd Finger Exercise

1. BEFORE YOU BEGIN,
   GET INTO SQUARE POSITIOIN,
   MAKE A **STOP** SIGN

2. DROP YOUR **AIRPLANE**
   TO THE E STRING

3. **TIK TOK** ELBOW
   TOWARDS THE E STRING

4. WALK YOUR
   FINGERS **1-2-3**

5. THEN PLAY...

REPEAT 4 TIMES

TAKE ONE FINGER OFF AT A TIME!

PASCALE METHOD

Lesson Eight
Theory
Review Test

Refer to the diagram :

1. What are the five lines called?(circle answer)

   ZEBRA STRIPES　　　**FIVE STIX**　　　**STAFF**

2. How many measures are there?_____

3. Circle the A note

4. Make an X on the E note

5. Color in the G note

6. Draw a smile on the D note

7. Draw any note on a line in the first measure.

8. Clrcle the repeat sign

9. Which one is a half note? (circle answer)

10. Which one is a quarter note?

11. How many beats or counts are in a half note?

    5　　　　**43**　　　　**2**

12. Which symbol means 'rest for two beats'?

13. Which symbol means down bow?

14. What direction is up bow?

    A) FROG TO FROG　　　**B) FROG TO TIP**　　　**C) TIP TO FROG**

15. What is another name for treble clef?

    SWIRBW　　　**G CLEF**　　　**B LINE**

16. What does pizzicato mean?

    FINISH　　　**PLUCK**　　　**EAT PIZZA**

PASCALE METHOD

?

If you answer 13 questions or more correctly, turn the page!

Lesson Nine

Memorizing Music, & Looking Ahead to Graduation

There are only four more lessons! If you are diligently practicing your assignments you should have no problem meeting your requirements for graduation. In this lesson we ask you to memorize "A Little Mozart." Try practicing in front of a mirror and keep an eye on your form.

Take Note!

we ♡ AWARDS

Stickers and badges work really well,

but every now and then a trip to the

toy store can add to the fun!!

PASCALE METHOD

Lesson Nine

Practice Assignment #9

_____ 1. Quickly, take the steps to **Hold Your Violin Correctly**. Try this short cut: 📹
    a) Start in _rest position_. Stick the _end button_ of your violin in your ear.
      Keep a **table position**.
    b) Drop your violin slowly down until it taps your shoulder.
    c) Lift your chin, head turns to look at the _scroll_, gently drop chin into the _chin rest_.

_____ 2. With your violin in playing position: 📹
    a) Do the **Elevator** ↕ (4x)   b) On the violin ↔ (2x each string)

_____ 3. **Find Your Shapes:** ☐ ◺ ☐ ◺ 📹
          Square Big Triangle Square Small Triangle

_____ 4. In **Square Position** and holding your **Stop Sign**, practice the **Airplane Wing** 📹
    on all of your strings. Remember, your hand and elbow stay together.

_____ 5. Play your open strings (4x). Use the whole bow (frog to tip). Feel each bow level.
    On the G, the bow is parallel to the floor. See the bow as a table. Imagine your
    favorite drink on the table. ☕
    If the bow angle dips, the drink will slide off!

_____ 6. **On and Off the Train** (Page C-6) 📹
    1a) With stops (3x) each string
    1b) Without stops (3x) each string

    Counting Train Cars
    2. Count 4 cars, 3 cars, 2 cars and 1 car (2x) each string

> A DROPPED RIGHT SHOULDER WILL LEVEL YOUR BOW

_____ 7. Place a _wrist helper_. Practice the **Four String Airplane**. 📹
    Play it slowly. Play it faster. Stay loose and tension free.

_____ 8. Practice your ____ scale. Choose a different scale each practice day!
    D scale (Page 5-3) Play each note 2x.
    A scale (Page 7-3) Play each note 4x using a faster _tempo_.
    G scale (Page 8-3) Play each note 1x using the whole bow (frog to tip).

_____ 9. Practice A Little Mozart, **3rd Finger Exercise.** (Page 8-4)

_____ 10. Practice A Little Mozart. (Page 9-4)

DAY 1	DAY 2	DAY 3	DAY 4	DAY 5	DAY 6	DAY 7

PASCALE METHOD

Lesson Nine
Mozart Factoids

WOLFGANG AMADEUS MOZART is considered one of the greatest classical music composers who has ever lived.

Born on January 27, 1756, he was baptized Johannes Chrysostomus Wolfgangus Theophilus Mozart. His nickname was "Wolfie."

Mozart never attended school. He and his sister, Maria Anna (nicknamed "Nannerl"), were home-schooled by their father, Leopold, who was a composer. Their mother, Anna Maria, bore seven children in all, but only Wolfie and Nannerl survived to adulthood.

The family dog was named Bumperl.

At the age of 2, it is said, Mozart identified a pig's squeal as a G sharp.

At 3, he began playing the clavinet, a keyboard instrument. At 4, he took up the violin.

He wrote music before he could write words. He composed his first musical piece at age five, his first minuet at 6, first symphony at 8, and first opera at 11.

When he was 6 years old, his parents took him and his sister, then 11, on tour all over Europe, playing as child prodigies. Their audiences included royal families. The Mozarts travelled by horse-drawn carriage and boat to the courts of London, Paris, The Hague, and Zurich.

In all, Mozart wrote over 600 pieces, a vast number, making him on of the world's most prolific composers.

PASCALE METHOD

Lesson Nine
Learn to Read
A Little Mozart #3

Fine!

PASCALE METHOD

Lesson Ten
Review & D Scale Challenge

This week, take the D Scale Challenge! Using your best form, play the D scale 10 times every day. Not only will you earn a badge for your effort, but you'll also build up strength and dexterity in your left hand needed for advancing technique.

Lots of review this week and attention to using correct form.

Take Note!

STUDENTS...

It's not how long
you practice,
but the quality of
your effort that counts.
Stay focused!

TAKE THE D SCALE CHALLENGE!

Lesson Ten

Practice Assignment #10

_____ 1. Quickly, take the short cut to hold your violin. 📷
   a) Start in *rest position*. Stick the *end button* of your violin in your ear.
      Keep a **Table Position**.
   b) Drop your violin slowly down until it taps your shoulder.
   c) Lift your chin, head turns to look at the *scroll*, drop chin into *chin rest*.

_____ 2. With your violin in playing position. 📷
   a) Do the **Elevator** ↕ (4x)   b) On the violin ↔ (2x each string)

_____ 3. From a **Square Position** play your open strings. (4x) 📷
   Use the whole bow (*frog to tip*). Feel each bow level.

_____ 4. Place a *wrist helper*. Practice the **Four String Airplane**. 📷
   Play it slowly (2X). Play it faster. Stay loose and tension free. EA | AD | DG
                                                                      EA | AD | DG

_____ 5. In **Square Position** and holding your **Stop Sign**, place your bow on the 📷
   sounding point and do the **Airplane Wing**. Find the **Table Position** on your G string.
   Posture: Stand tall. Shoulders relaxed. Remember, hand and elbow stay together.

_____ 6. **On and Off the Train** (Page C-6) 📷
   1a) With stops (2x) each string
   1b) Without stops (2x) each string

   check for tension

_____ 7. **Counting Train Cars** (Page C-6) 📷
   Count 4 cars, 3 cars, 2 cars and 1 car (1x) on each string. Start with G.

_____ 8. D Scale Challenge: Play your scale 70x this week. Keep track below.
   Meet the challenge and reward yourself with a badge!

D SCALE CHALLENGE	→							
		1	2	3	4	5	6	7

WINNERS EARN A BADGE!

_____ 9. Practice A Little Mozart, **3rd Finger Exercise.** (Page 8-4)

_____ 10. Practice A Little Mozart #3. (Page 9-4)

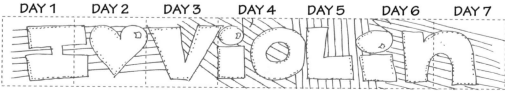

DAY 1   DAY 2   DAY 3   DAY 4   DAY 5   DAY 6   DAY 7

PASCALE METHOD

Lesson Eleven

Home Stretch & Taking Stock

Next week is your last class and final exam. In this lesson you are given an opportunity to review the basic violin skills needed to graduate. Be sure to practice each numbered exercise and check off each one every day. Go back and review the exercises you still need help with and be sure to refer to the DVD!

Take Note!

Kids who play
together like to
PLAY TOGETHER!

Find a friend
to practice with.

PASCALE METHOD

Lesson Eleven
Practice Assignment #11

Check off each exercise as you practice every day. When you feel you've mastered the exercise, using good form and a relaxed disposition, place a check mark or *finger pal* sticker in the circle.

For the final exam you should be able to:

_____ 1. **Hold Your Violin Correctly** and comfortably.

_____ 2. Hold your bow using the **Train Gang** steps. Say them out loud.

_____ 3. Place your fingers **On and Off the Train**.

_____ 4. Find **Square Position** on **The Wall** and demonstrate each bow level. Use any rhythm pattern.

_____ 5. **Find Your Shapes.**

_____ 6. **Count Train Cars** (4x) and (2x) on any string.

_____ 7. Play whole bows while you **Look at your Watch** (bend your wrist).

_____ 8. Identify your 4 Basic Notes and play them on your violin (refer to your flash cards).

_____ 9. Line up your **Stop Sign**, and Tik Tok to each string, **Walking Your Fingers** 1-2-3.

_____ 10. Do the **Four String Airplane** exercise. Start on your E string.

_____ 11. Play the G scale, D scale or A scale. Use your first *finger pal* and **Find Your Y** to keep your fingers tall.

_____ 12. Using your **4 Step Left Hand**, play A Little Mozart from memory.

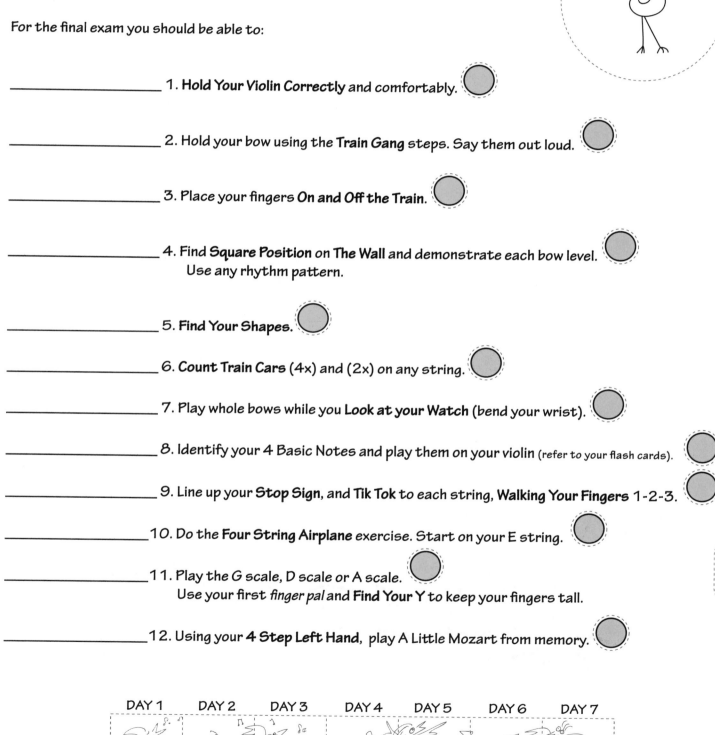

| DAY 1 | DAY 2 | DAY 3 | DAY 4 | DAY 5 | DAY 6 | DAY 7 |

PASCALE METHOD

Lesson Twelve
Final Exam

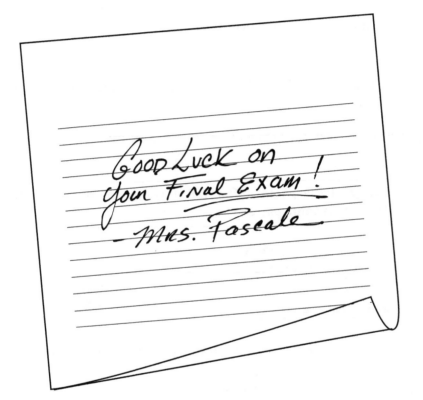

Good Luck on Your Final Exam!
— Mrs. Pascale

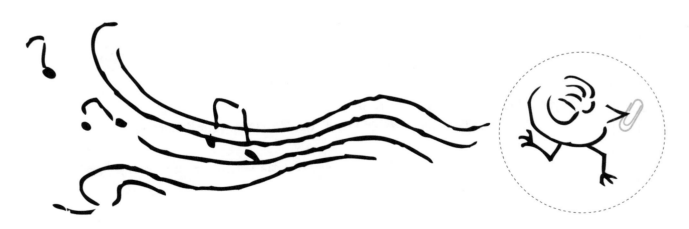

PASCALE METHOD

Lesson Twelve

Final Exam

Demonstrate the following for your teacher.
Don't have a teacher? Email a video to finalexam@PascaleMethod.com

For the final exam you should be able to:

Points Earned

1. Take steps to **Hold Your Violin** correctly and comfortably (5 points).................... ☐

2. Hold your bow saying the **Train Gang** steps out loud. (5 points)..................... ☐

3. Demonstrate **On and Off the Train** (with stops) on the G string and (without stops) on the D string. (5 points)................... ☐

4. From **Square Position, Find Your Shapes** on your D and A strings. (5 points)........................ ☐

5. Demonstrate the **Two String Airplane** exercise. Start on your E string. (5 points)............. ☐

6. Play a D scale using your best form. (20 points)... ☐

7. Using your **4 Step Left Hand**, and the technique you learned from the Third Finger Exercise (Page 8-4), play A Little Mozart (Page 9-4) from memory. (50 points)........................... ☐

8. Identify the following: (1 point each).. ☐

♩   𝄽   ⊓   ▬   ♫

___   ___   ___   ___   ___

IF YOU SCORED 70 POINTS OR MORE YOU PASSED!

Total Points: _____

Passed ☐   Retake the Course ☐

Twelve

PASCALE METHOD

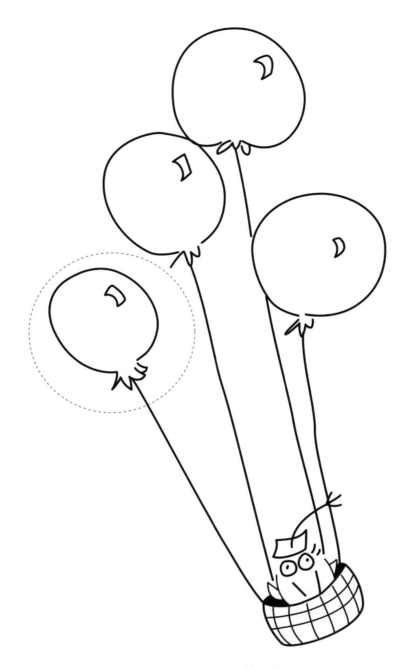

Congratulations
Graduate!

Certificate of Completion

THIS AWARD IS PRESENTED TO:

FOR SUCCESSFULLY COMPLETING

PASCALE METHOD®

FOR Beginning violin

Awarded this _____ day of _____, 20 _____

the Pascale Method

MR. CONDUCTOR PRESENTS...

PASCALE METHOD

Let's imagine...

...that your bow is a train and your fingers are travelers

on the train. Each traveler has a special role to play on

the train and all of them will help you stay on track!

INTRODUCING...
The Train Gang

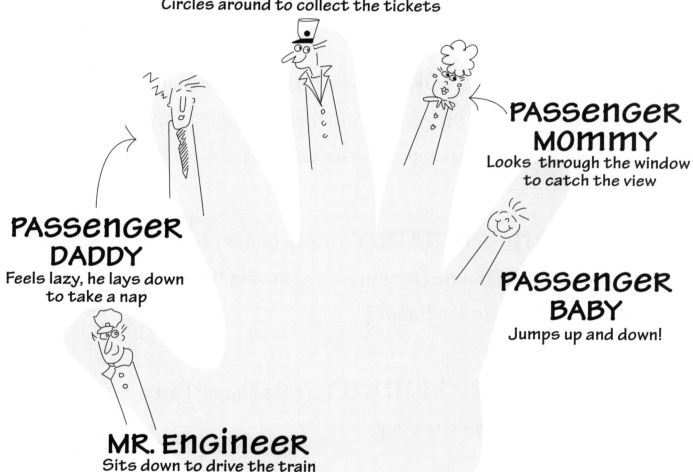

MR. CONDUCTOR
Circles around to collect the tickets

PASSENGER MOMMY
Looks through the window to catch the view

PASSENGER DADDY
Feels lazy, he lays down to take a nap

PASSENGER BABY
Jumps up and down!

MR. ENGINEER
Sits down to drive the train

PASCALE METHOD

Train Gang Bow Hold

PASSENGERS TAKE THEIR PLACES ON THE TRAIN

Hold the bow stick with your left hand and do the five steps of this exercise.

1. **MR. ENGINEER** (thumb) sits down to drive the train. (Make sure it's bent and leaning against the bow hair.)

2. **MR. CONDUCTOR** (middle finger) circles around to collect the tickets. He stops to visit Mr. Engineer. Careful, don't sit on his head! (Keep right of the thumb.)

3. **PASSENGER DADDY** (index finger) feels lazy. He lays down to take a nap. (Be sure to rest the finger on the *second phalanx* of the index finger.)

4. **PASSENGER MOMMY** (ring finger) looks through the window to catch the view.

5. **PASSENGER BABY** (pinky finger) jumps up and down! (AKA Pinky Push - ups)

PASCALE METHOD

Elevator &
Elevator on the Violin (see video)

BENT WRIST = STRAIGHT BOW = GREAT SOUND!

---

1. MAKE A GOOD BOW

Turn the bow hairs to face your nose.

2. MOVE THE BOW UP AND DOWN

Lead with your wrist.

3. LOOK FOR THE ∩'S AND ∪'S

(The shape you are making with your wrist.)

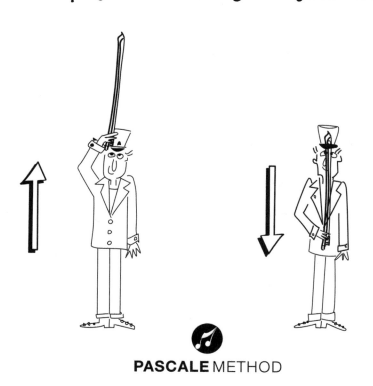

On and Off the Train
&
Counting Train Cars

Directions:

Place Mr. Engineer, Mr. Conductor, and the three passengers on the train (bow) one by one. When they are all in place, practice the following bow hand exercises:

1a. On AND OFF THE TRAIN (with stops)

Start with all fingers on the bow. Travel, then stop. At each station a passenger gets off the train. Last stop is at the tip. Each passenger then gets back on the train one at a time, until you return back to the frog.

1b. On AND OFF THE MOVING TRAIN (without stops)

Same exercise as #1, except keep the train moving. Rememember to travel, then lift (each finger).

2. Counting Train Cars

As you pull your bow, divide it into equal parts.

- Count 4 cars

- Count 3 cars

- Count 2 cars

- Count 1 car

Frog   Tip

PASCALE METHOD

GO TO
The Wall
FOR GREAT FORM!

1. FIND A WALL

2. SQUARE OFF

'Glue' your shoulder, elbow, and left shoulder to your wall. Place your bow where the center dot meets the sounding point.

3. PLAY

Starting on the G string, play ⊓ & V bows on each string. Stay in the *middle bow* area.

4. TRAVEL

Using your **Airplane Wing**, and keeping your bow on the *center dot*, travel from the G to E string. Feel each bow level as you drop from the forearm. (Elbow and hand stay together.)

Choose a chant:

"I love to play my vi-o-lin"

"I love choc-late ice-cream"

Make one up!

Glossary

PASCALE METHOD FOR Beginning Violin

The exercises listed in bold below are all demonstrated on the accompanying DVD.

Airplane Wing: The motion your right arm makes when the bow travels from string to string in **Square Position**. It is motored by the forearm.

Back Button: Extension of the back of the violin. (See Page 1-3)

Center Dots: Small stickers found on every Sticker Buddies page, used to mark the point on the bow stick where your right arm forms a square. (See **Square Position**.) Dots may also be used to mark bow division.

Chin Rest: A part of the violin (See Page 1-3)

Elevator: A bow exercise found in The Caboose, in which the bow is raised and lowered close to the body, with the bow hair facing the nose. This motion teaches bending the wrist, which is necessary for a straight bow and good sound. (Page C-5)

Elevator on the Violin: Based on the motion learned in the **Elevator**, the student draws the bow horizontally on the violin.

End Button: (See Page 1-3)

Find Your Shapes: Bow arm exercise whereby shapes are created when travelling from **Square Position** to the tip, back to **Square Position**, and then to the frog.

Find Your Y: The letter that appears on a child's hand when they bend their first finger.

Fingerboard: A part of the violin (See Page 1-3)

Fingers Lay in Sun: The second step of the **4 Step Left Hand**, where the fingers lay back at a 45 degree angle.

Finger Pal: Also called Moody **Finger Pals**. These are the face stickers found on every Sticker Buddies page. Finger Pals are placed on the index fingernail, to help the left hand position. Match your mood to a pal!

Finger Table: The shape your finger forms when you circle your first finger down from a **Stop Sign** to **Find Your Y**.

First Finger Goes to the Gym: A strength training exercise, in which the first finger moves up and down on the first tape.

PASCALE METHOD

Glossary

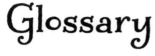

Frog:	A part of the bow. (See Page 2-3)
4 Step Left Hand:	A four-step process for setting up the left hand.
Four String Airplane:	This exercise promotes a good, relaxed bow arm by dropping the arm; swinging to the next string level; then bending the wrist. (See **Two String Airplane**)
Hold Your Violin Correctly:	Refers to taking the eight steps.
Intonation:	Playing in tune.
Lay in Sun:	The second step of the **4 Step Left Hand**, where the fingers lay back at a 45 degree angle.
Look at Your Watch:	The position of the wrist when bowing towards the frog.
Make Your Violin a Table:	Placement of the violin is parallel to the floor.
Middle Bow:	A part of the bow. (See Page 2-3)
On and Off the Train:	Exercise found in The Caboose (Page C -6) for bow finger placement.
Pinky Push-ups:	Strength training exercise for the bow hand pinky (lifts up and down).
Pizzicato:	Plucking the strings.
Pluck:	Also called pizzicato. The thumb rests on the corner of the fingerboard and the first finger circles around, creating a doorway. Then pull the string with the padded part of the fingertip.
Scroll:	A part of the violin (See Page 1-3).
Sleeping Hand:	A relaxed hand position.
Sounding Point:	Bow placement on the string between the bridge and the fingerboard, where violinists find their fullest sound.
Square Position:	A starting position in which the middle of the bow is placed on the sounding point.
Stop Sign:	A starting left hand position where the bottom of the index finger (third crease down) lines up with the bottom of the *fingerboard*. Fingers point to the ceiling.

Glossary

Table Position: Placement of the violin when the player is in square position, and the violin is parallel to the floor. (The violin is level enough that it can balance an invisible coffee cup.)

Tempo: How fast or slow something is played.

The Wall: Exercise found in The Caboose, which promotes a good bow arm from the beginning.

Tik Tok: Exercise in which the left wrist and forearm move in and out as one unit.

Time Signature: An indication of rhythm resembling a fraction. The top number tells us the number of beats in each measure. The bottom number tells us the division of the whole note.

Train Gang: Characters representing the five bow hand fingers. Meet them at The Caboose.

Two String Airplane: This exercise, done on the E and A string, promotes a good, relaxed bow arm. Drop the arm; swing to the next string level; then pull the bow while bending the wrist. (See also the **Four String Airplane.**)

Up Bow ('V'): Bow motion traveling from the tip to the frog.

Walk Your Fingers: To place fingers 1, 2, 3 on the fingerboard, using the **4 Step Left Hand**.

Walk Your Fingers, Start With One To place your first finger on the G,D,A and E strings using the **4 Step Left Hand**.

Wrist Helper: A sticker affixed to the center top of the wrist, used as a reminder to lead with your wrist when the bow is travelling from the tip to the frog. Found on the Sticker Buddies pages.